Lima :: Limón

Also by Natalie Scenters-Zapico
The Verging Cities

Lima :: Limón

Natalie Scenters-Zapico

Copper Canyon Press
Port Townsend, Washington

Cover art: Harry Gamboa Jr., *À la Mode*, 1976, from the Asco era; ©1976, Harry Gamboa Jr.; 16 inches × 20 inches, gelatin silver print; edition of ten. Smithsonian American Art Museum. Museum purchase through the Luisita L. and Franz H. Denghausen Endowment.

Copper Canyon Press is in residence at Fort Worden State Park in Port Townsend, Washington, under the auspices of Centrum. Centrum is a gathering place for artists and creative thinkers from around the world, students of all ages and backgrounds, and audiences seeking extraordinary cultural enrichment.

LIBRARY OF CONGRESS CATALOGING-IN-PUBLICATION DATA
Names: Scenters-Zapico, Natalie, author.
Title: Lima : Limon / Natalie Scenters-Zapico.
Description: Port Townsend, Washington : Copper Canyon Press, [2019] |
    Includes bibliographical references.
Identifiers: LCCN 2018048964 | ISBN 9781556595318 (paperback : alk. paper)
Subjects: LCSH: American poetry—Mexican American authors. | American
    poetry—Women authors. | American poetry—21st century.
Classification: LCC PS3619.C285 A6 2019 | DDC 811/.6—dc23
LC record available at https://lccn.loc.gov/2018048964

9 8 7 6 5 4 3 2 FIRST PRINTING

Copper Canyon Press
Post Office Box 271
Port Townsend, Washington 98368

www.coppercanyonpress.org

This book is for
my sister, Elaine,
& my mother, Clara,
who taught me to create life;

::

my abuelita, Marxina,
& my bisabuela, Felicidad,
who predicted their own deaths.

CONTENTS

::

::

Lima :: Limón

Y los niños cantan a la rueda, rueda
Esta triste copla que el viento le lleva.
A la lima y al limón,
Tú no tienes quien te quiera.
A la lima y al limón,
Te vas quedar soltera.
Que penita y que dolor.
Que penita y que dolor,
La vecinita de enfrente soltera se quedó.

::

& the children sing round & round
This sad copla that the wind takes
From the lemon to the lime,
You have no one to love you.
From the lemon to the lime,
You will end up single.
What pain & what shame.
What pain & what shame,
The little neighbor girl from in front ended up single.

Conchita Piquer, "Lima Limón"

Lima Limón :: Infancia

I want to be the lemons in the bowl
on the cover of the magazine. I want
to be round, to be yellow, to be pulled

from branches. I want to be wax, to be
white with pith, to be bright, to be zested
in the corners of a table. I want you

to say my name like the word: lemon.
Say it like the word: limón. Undress me
in strands of rind. I want my saliva to be

citrus. I want to corrode my husband's
wedding ring. I want to be a lemon
with my equator marked in black ink—
small dashes to show my shape: pitted & convex.

Neomachismo

To see if you're still alive, heat caramel in a pan until it spits asteroids on your arms. Take good care of your burns. Your scars should never last longer than two years. Pain needs a clean slate to play on.

Wear a red dress & let men pull at it all night. Your desire: to have your hair pulled, to bleed, to lick your wounds like a dog in heat.

Say you're sorry for getting angry. Say you're sorry for being angry. Say you're sorry that you're angry.

Anger is the emotion of men. By adding sugar, lime & salt you can turn anger into sadness as a good woman should.

Stop sobbing, it's ugly. Instead, emulate the glass tears on virgins who look up to the men who bruised their bodies.

Tell your man: *You're machista.* Have him repeat this statement back to you in html.

Like in the movies let the pot boil over, until he screams he'll send you back home to your mother. When he can't stop laughing, laugh too— become the foreigner who doesn't understand.

¡Ay pena penita pena! Listen to Lola Flores & search for the pain between your eyes on WebMD. Don't feel bad if you sob in one room while he reads about aporia in the next.

Like la Lola Flores, you have beautiful hair; unlike la Lola, sell it to make rent.

Laugh when he says: Mi'ja, cabróna, ingrata & eres mía. Assure him he's not turning into his father.

When he says you are letting this happen, don't reply. Put his fingers in your mouth & hold your breath when he asks: *Who taught you to hate yourself?*

In the Age of Los Zetas

Saint Michael hangs demons
with velvet thread & opens
a torrent of tissue flames

in a scene created in a box
of Altoids. Saint Michael bites
a cracked enamel heart,

too big for his tiny
plastic cleft to carry.
I am in mourning

in the bloodiest year
of Mexican history. I stare
at Saint Michael, my little

automaton, & feed myself
week-old bread that crumbles
my teeth to dirt. I save my oral

rubble to sell as earth
for the burial of men.
Men who only value

a woman for her extra rib,
that holy thing that breaks
& heals without a cast.

Men who want to fill
my body with a clutter
of spiders, eager to eat the flies

that swarm my uterine lining.
In the age of Los Zetas, I only take
what I can carry: a reliquary

of clots—all the children
I've failed to bear because
I've been hit by men who

in their thirst for me, strangled
a flash flood into our kitchen.
Don't tell me I deserve better

in the age of Los Zetas. I am blessed
with a man as beautiful
as Saint Michael, whose shirts

I pierce, tug & embroider
with roses made from a demon's
noosed velvet thread.

Lima Limón :: Azahar

I lie on my back in the grass & let the weight
of a man on top of me. Out of breath, he searches
for a place on my body that hasn't flooded.
The only dry patch left is my hair, which he uses
to wipe the sweat from his face. He is disgusted
because I have turned the earth beneath us
damp. He says I am an experience, like standing
in an irrigated grove of lemon trees. He says
I am the water pooled at each trunk, infused
with citrus & pesticide. He says my moisture
brings mold & my body is nauseating.
I wonder if I had not said his name over & over
would he still think of me as small & round
& fresh as lemon—as vaginal & arched as limón.

At a Party I Tell a Story & Ask:

Isn't that funny? I've yet to find
someone who laughs. Instead,
people observe me for a sign
of how a man could have been
mistaken. How he could have
pulled his car next to me & asked:
How much? Why I responded:
No, I'm sorry. It's like the opening
of *Butterfield 8* with blood
instead of lipstick: No Sale. It's how
I screamed at my last blood test
because my blood drew black
for lack of iron. The nurse:
What is your diet? Cardboard
& batteries. *& your mother's?*
Ink & bullets. *& your father's?*
Hat pins & terraria. In my pocket,
a peso I thumb hoping to change
it for a dollar. I run from man
to man. They are all kissing behind
glass doors asking for an exchange:
A dollar for this peso, just one dollar.
I run to the park searching
for a dolarero. *Will you give
me a dollar, just one dollar, for a peso?*
There's no dolarero & I'm left
running with a peso in my hand.
I didn't die in the park & where
I'm from it's a blessing not to be
a woman gagged by electrical tape
& bound to the hood of a car.
My death wish: a grain of sand
will kill me & I will be born again

as a crab scuttling across
a kitchen table, paid for by a peso
that could afford my delicate legs.

I Am à la Mode

Using a No. 2 pencil I circle the vein under my right eye, the scar from a sore on my upper lip, an arrow to show how my left ear sticks out more than my right. I want to correct all that prevents me from becoming divine, appear to every man like a virgin apparition in the flesh. I powder my face to glow, pinch the saggy skin under my eyes until I cry. I repeat: it's good to look sad, it's good to look, it's good.

I heat bobby pins with a lighter & use them to brand little loops across my wrists. I name the scars after angels: Michael, Gabriel, Rafael. I don't want to die, I just want to look sad. I want to cry tears so perfect they are made of glass. I stuff each finger into a black glove & belt my man's shirt for all the times my mother called me marimacha. I climb on top of the kitchen table & say: *I am el rey & you are mi reina & all of this mi reyno.* My brother sets up a camera to capture this, then stands in a corner, leans against a wall with his hands in his pockets. I call my man *Mi reina* over & over.

My Macho Takes Care of Me Good

because he's a citizen de los united estates.
I got a stove this big, a refri this full, a mirror
just to see my pretty face. He says:

My name's on this license. I drive la troca,
so you don't have to, mi'ja. I am a citizen
de los united estates. Because he's a citizen,

we are muy lejos de dios, but we love
los united estates. I don't wash laundry with cakes
of Jabón Zote, because my macho

takes care of me good. I bring my macho
Nescafé, American made, because he's a citizen
de los united estates. I ask for feria to go to a doctor,

& he says: *Ingrata, you're not sick.*
I clean chiles, then rub my eyes—
¡Siempre llora-lloras, chillona!

& he's right, I lloro-lloro sin saber
por qué. I bring my macho smoke in a glass
& smooth every shirt with my new electric iron.

He says: *No hay nadie en casa. ¿Why wear*
clothes at all? So I don't. I fry chicharrones.
Hiss-hiss, across my bare skin. *Bang-bang,*

my macho's fists on the table. He wants más, más,
y más in his united estates. I give him all of me
served on a platter from back home:

plump, cracked & ready-made. *Crunch-crunch,*
eats my macho. *You married him,* says my mother,
& he takes care of you good in his united estates.

Lima Limón :: Madurez

I wear a peineta & pin a mantilla to my hair
I want to be Conchita Piquer warning women
about becoming lemons. The goal: tener alguien

quien me quiera. I want to be my mother singing me
to sleep: *A la lima y al limón, te vas quedar soltera.*
My grandmother hated peinetas, mantillas & women

who wore too much gold. She'd say this pulling my hair
tight into a bun. She hated peinetas & mantillas:
Pero la necesidad obliga. I don't want to be the woman

whose skin dissolves into the caldos she makes
for her dying parents. That kind of woman cries alone
because she has no fat husband to make her cry

in a home of her own. A la lima y al limón, tú no tienes
quien te quiera. A la lima y al limón, te vas quedar soltera.

Women's Work

I embroider the days of the lunar
        calendar on handkerchiefs to track
                my menstrual omissions. The only way

        to catch a stray breath is by exhaling
on glass & releasing from its cage
        the river that lives among pulsing

                cilia. I place a TV, the size of my palm,
        between my legs & by its glare see
a moonless night. I laugh at the thought

        of burglary, stitch a cigar under
                an apple tree on my belly, fall
        asleep to the soft sound of thread

tugging on skin & wish my grandmother
        could show me how to wash my feet
                with a bucket of sand & a kettle

        of hot water. I work to make
my body a comfort. My body:
        the table where strangers sit to be served

                as king in a court of cross-stitched
        felons. Each felon with a needle's prick
assassins down the highway of my legs.

                An eyelash is pressed taut against fabric
        & I know my body is a sutured thing,
which by my hand can be torn & with a needle stitched again.

He Has an Oral Fixation

He can't stop putting the dead
flowers, the dead-head nails, the dead weight
sacks of flour, in his mouth. He can't
stop writing about the mouth. The way

he woke up to his mouth full of bees,
their dead crunch still stinging
his gums. He writes: *There's something*
beautiful in the way a mouth can be broken

by saliva & cold air. She broke
his mouth open & filled it with lead-
tainted earth. She made him
brain-dead through the mouth;

licked the honey she pulled
from his incisors like sap from a tree.
His mouth, with its stretch marks
running along each cheek—she's never seen

anything like it. His mouth a scar
of his hunger, a scar of his gluttony
after the hunger. Stop writing
about the mouth: the teeth, the gums,

the impacted tooth & its psychedelic
blues & greens. Stop writing how she bit
your mouth & with a blowtorch
welded its dark-open shut. Stop writing

about the mouth: the tongue, the holy
molars, the wear of grinding yourself
to bone. Stop writing about the mouth:
his mouth, your mouth, her mouth.

Lima Limón :: Vejez

My body is a frutería where wives send
their husbands to ask for a dozen limones.
I pull at the fat around my waist & unravel

a plastic bag. I count each limón from the bin
between my ribs & feel for the juice under
thin skin. Each husband takes a piece of my body

home with him in every limón. A piece of my body
he can slice into quarters & squeeze into
his beer. A piece of my body to press into sugar

& feed to his children laughing at the TV. What more
can I give than my body in pieces to strange husbands?
What more can I give than the limones that grow

between my breasts? I tell each husband:
¡Ay limón, mi limonero! Show me your list.

Sonnet for a Dollar

You tied the boy's shoes every morning.
You washed his desk with shaving cream.
You opened your mouth & let him look inside.
You kicked teacher in the shin & said: *Sorry, Miss.*

You kissed him on the lips for five seconds.
You gave him shivers. You gave him the knife.
You read books in a whisper, close to his face.
You let him slap you, then rock you in his arms.

You let him unclasp your bra with his eyes closed.
You let him call you puta in front of his friends.
You let him bite your finger until it turned purple.
You crawled on your hands & knees like a dog.

When you told your father all the things you'd done
for a dollar, he laughed & laughed.

Kept

I was so thirsty, you cracked
an egg into my mouth. I ate it
& thanked you. We were so

rich then. I imagined the moon,
a being I'd never seen, in every nail
you'd use to tack the tarp

over our heads. I confused
hens clucking for the ringing
of the phone you'd never

let me answer. With a spatula
to my ear, I'd pretend to be
a woman on TV & say:

¿Bueno? Your anger
was the gun you kept by the door,
my fear, the knife I used to chop

onions. One night you confused
the sound of a snake rattling
for rain. The snake opened

its jaw & its fangs were the color
of mud. You reached for my thighs
just before you died & I couldn't

face you. Once you stopped
breathing I rubbed your beard
between my hands

& played the most beautiful
cumbia. We danced
for the first time since our wedding.

Discovery

Her knees are caves, her belly
home to a colony

of snakes. I draw maps
of lands she's never seen

on the palms of her hands.
My arms, a river

that floods her throat. Her thirst,
a tongue washed

with charcoal. Say: *Help.*
She will show me how

to harvest the roots
of any tree. Say: *Sky.*

I'll pinch every inch
of her skin. I named her

America, because I own
her body & her child's.

Every river down her arms
I must rename. When I got

the cartography wrong
I said: *Tear the map*

in half so we won't
get confused. America's hands

bled & bled. I told her:
Clean it up.

I Didn't Know You Could Buy

something not for sale until
I walked through Coyoacán
& watched gringos ignore

sign after sign: Casa No En Venta.
Still I watched men knock
on door after door stalking

houses they could paint blue,
just like Frida Kahlo's. It's like
the time two thieves knocked me

to my knees for twenty dollars.
I thought the thieves jewelers
as they punched my jaw until

each tooth turned dark amber.
Later, to save my body, I set
my teeth, muddy stones, into a crown

I wore the rest of summer. I know
how to hide bruises so the earth
won't get jealous of lightning

produced by simple friction.
My landscape of curves & edges
that breaks light spectral

is not for sale, but men still knock
on rib after rib, stalking the perfect house—
the perfect shade of blue.

Lima Limón :: Decrepitud

When the stranger learns I speak Spanish
he makes me stand in my underwear & read
from Borges's *El Aleph*. & because I only want
the stranger to love me, I read & wonder if Borges
could help me jump through a period on the page
to my death. After, the stranger whispers:
You are lima, your tongue strips ink from pages. I wonder
if the stranger imagines lima as green or yellow,
as sweet or bitter—or as a city where the snow
collects on your lover's eyelashes in mid-July.

Say limón: clean & ripe & bursting on your tongue.
Say lemon: broken & ugly & not up to par.
Say lima: Rimak & rima & spoken from God.

God speaks. Rima. Rimak. God has spoken.
Rimak. Rima. Lemon. Lima. Limón.

Te vas porque yo quiero que te vayas.
A la hora que yo quiera te detengo.
Yo sé que mi cariño te hace falta
Porque quieras o no yo soy tu dueño.

::

You go because I want you to go.
At the time I want you, I'll stop you.
I know that you miss my affection
Because like it or not, I am your master.

José Alfredo Jiménez, "La Media Vuelta"

Macho :: Hembra

I cleaned chiles until my fingers burned to feed him. Like my father did to my mother at parties, he called me tontita. When we danced, I pressed my body against his. He smiled & pet my head like a dog. A good hembra never speaks of the violence of men.

She Is à la Mode

A sheet cake soaked in milk & left suspended. She had no decorations, so she placed a sugar bowl on top. She placed her man at the head of the cake & told him to close his eyes & relax: *Lean back, mi rey, you deserve comfort at the head of my cake.* She wanted to capture the cake before it was consumed, so she called her brother-in-law & asked him to stand behind the cake for good balance. She jumped on top of the cake, folded her legs like Minnie Mouse & told everyone to be cool, this cake was going to be in a movie. She was going to call it À la Mode & this was to be the opening scene. *But there's no ice cream,* her man said. *No, my body is the ice cream,* she said & pursed her lips for the camera until her mouth became a dark wound. Her man, who adored her again for a minute, said: *You're so dumb, clean up this kitchen already, da asco.* She waited for the hot water to run & poured a cap full of bleach in the sink. She cried: *All my movies are no movies. All my movies are not mine.*

My Gift

I run around the block eating an orange & drop
its rind in continents on concrete. This is my gift
to the suburb, which told me not to burn logs

when the air quality is marked yellow. My dog
chases me around the block barking & a woman
yells from her portrait window she could sue me

for not using a leash. My phone reminds me to take
a shower, so I do. It's not that I'm dirty, it's that
I'd rather stay in bed wearing fur, watching

documentaries about Dior. I apologize to no one
while scrubbing my scalp until it bleeds. I know
what it is to stare at yourself in a shattered mirror

& not remember if it was you who broke it.
I wanted to see if I could mine my body for rubies
& look, I can! I write a letter & don't send it:

Here is a book & a ruby. One from my body,
the other I made after a fit with a pen. Both
worth nothing, but I like the thought of a man
picking them up & holding them in his hands.

Macho :: Hembra

I laughed because, after all, isn't that what women do—laugh at jokes at
their own expense? I was his pocha hermosa. He'd done good because
of my fair skin & green eyes. He liked keeping me in my underwear in
his room. Like a porcelain doll come to life, I was the perfect object.
I screamed & was ashamed. He'd hand me matches & I'd strike each
one against my teeth to make a flame. I'd whisper in his ear bruto &
he'd hush me with the word hocicona. I'd cry & he'd kiss me quiet. My
whole face fit in his cupped hands. He was el macho :: I was la hembra.
To clean his body I'd blow smoke from my cigarette on his shoulders.
I told myself I had found un buen macho. He was mi cielo: sky of my
many deaths.

Aesthetic Translation

The statistics speak for themselves.

I learned to read by sounding out the names
in obituaries of those who had died. There were
so many people I could never finish

the section before leaving for school.
Six women are murdered a day. Obituaries:
proof you can only die once. Six more

women will die today, six more
women will die tomorrow.
w: wo: wom: wome: women-women-women

. . . 95 percent of the murders in Juárez
are not investigated . . .

My room was a palace of stickers
& small stuffed toys. Because I could only leave
the house with a man, I never left

the house. Not because it was dangerous,
but because my parents couldn't
remember whether I knew how to swim,

even the desert floods in July
erasing all proof. Charles Bowden says:

The poor bastards
are being ground up since the day
they were born.

I am a poor bastard, who licks
the dirt from under her nails.
Dirt ground by the same beetles

that eat people in their makeshift
graves. Femicide,

Charles Bowden wrote, was an hembra
lie about machos—a myth.
Years later, Charles Bowden

would speak for Mexican women
of the violence of machos,
of femicide, for glossy magazines

far away. Charles Bowden:
collector of violence
against hembras. He won't let women

speak. Even after death, he
depends on the desert's shroud.

Whatever lesson Juárez holds
for México remains
elusive, as México's struggle

with lawlessness continues
to evolve. The mourning

doves gather on lampposts searching
for any pool of water to clean

their brown, pointed
beaks. The mourning doves eat
loose change

on streets. The mourning doves
open their wings & clean the air

of the maquila's smog. I breathe

deep, I breathe so deeply. I swear

I've died. I swear I was born

dead again.

He Finds a Kissing Bug

on my eyelid & says it is a tiny
curse from the nopal. I ask him why
it cursed me & he says, *You ate*

the nopal's fruit & licked your fingers.
He smashes the bug between
two fingers & throws it

in a plastic cup. It floats
on half-melted ice. He smashes it
against the cup's side until

the blood it took from me pinks
the water. *The kissing bug is mad,*
he says, *you stole the fruit from its mother*

so it wanted to steal from you.
I laugh & dab concealer to cover
the swelling. I think of the rats' eyes,

sharp cameras tracking my theft.
They sent the kissing bug to show you,
he says, *the smallest theft*

is the swelling of an eye. I close
my eyes & run my fingers across
each lid. I imagine the red dot rising until

I can't see. With a spoon I rescue
what's left of the kissing bug & kiss it—
the way the kissing bug kissed me.

More Than One Man Has Reached Up My Skirt

I've stopped asking:

                    ¿Why?
        I've let a man whistle
                from the table for more beer
& brought it to him
                with a smile. I've slapped
a man & ran
                while he laughed—
        atrevida.
I've had a miscarriage. I've let a man
                        kiss me
after an abortion
                        & comforted his hot tears.
I've done these things,
                    while other girls
work in maquilas
                piecing together
Dell computer boards,
                    while other girls
work in brothels,
                & cake foundation across
their bruised arms,
                    while other girls
            ride the bus home alone
        at night, every night,
while other girls are found
        wearing clothes
                that don't belong to them, or no
clothes at all. I've done all of this
                    while other girls are found
            with puta
                    written in blood across
their broken bellies.
        My mother used to cover
    my eyes

when we'd walk by girls
working the corner
    & say:

        See how lucky you are,
not to have to work
        like they do? I have been
    muy puta,

        have been called puta.
Yes, I'd say, *very lucky.*

Ixmiquilpan, Hidalgo, México

1

Part of the simulation is not knowing
your coyote's real name. Part of the simulation
is knowing your group could leave you
behind. Part of the simulation is knowing
that if you are left behind, a pickup truck
will take you back to your hotel.

2

Through caves, through brush, through needles
we form a line by holding on
to a stranger's backpack. In the dark live
rounds are fired. I duck, people laugh.

3

The desert here is no desert at all & I think of how
I could cut a thick barrel cactus open
& eat it. In Chihuahua I've never seen
thick barrel cactus, only the thin long threads
of ocotillo that don't carry much water.

4

The chairos pay 250 pesos to walk
all night in the desert in the middle of México
to simulate a border crossing. They bring jugs
filled with water & pose for selfies.

5

When you wade across the river you only have to worry
about swimming if a current pulls you under, not the red
glare of night-vision goggles, floodlights & guns.

6

In the simulation, only two people make it
to *the other side* without getting stopped by actors
portraying la migra or narcos. All are brought back
for cups of atole. *It's three in the morning,* a girl laughs.

7

I walk back to my room, turn on the light
& the flying ants won't stop swarming. It is so dark
& I have so much water left in my jug.
My teeth full of grit from the atole.

Macho :: Hembra

One night, I was done playing hembra. I asked him to stop playing macho. He pulled me by the arm to the side of the house. With one hand across my mouth, an arm across my shoulders & the weight of his body he repeatedly beat my head against brick until a faucet of blood opened from my head down my back. The pain became a vibration through my body. His hands :: death wish. Too weak to move, I slid down the wall & stared at a colony of ants that wound their way around my feet. I couldn't feel the ants pinching welts into my skin. He kneeled down to hold me & kiss my sweaty face. I wanted to be a good hembra. I let him hold me. I whispered: *Sorry, I'm sorry.* I got up & only wanted to shower. It is shameful to let a man touch you that way. It is even more shameful to speak it.

In the Culture of Now

My mother is dying of too much electricity on the brain, my father a limp in his walk & my macho lost his green card at a bus station. I want words split letter for letter to turn sound into wisdom on my losses.

::

My macho says: *Your skin is the color of milk, you glow between sheets.* ¿Who gives more light: me, or the luna lunera? Too much milk makes you sick—drink, drink, cascabelera.

::

I want to leave my hembra behind. ¿What are my options? She bleeds on the rug, births a litter, then hides limp bodies in kitchen cabinets.

::

I lied. My father is dying of too much electricity on the brain, my macho a limp in his walk & my mother lost her green card at a bus station. Whom these losses happened to matters to no one but me. To others, my loss is only worth its sum parts.

::

I pour a shot to get the flies drunk. Watch their little legs stagger. I like the flies tipsy, like my macho likes me when I am glazed on the kitchen floor, begging him not to leave me.

::

Come, kill me over the stove, under the running showerhead, gravel my skin bloody. I am so afraid one night my macho will choke me to death, though I am not afraid of dying.

::

My macho says: *Hembra, I imagine the woman I love when I'm with you, but you're not that woman.* I ask: *Who is she?* My macho says: *Cállate, take off your dress.* Each of his fingers strokes death. I only want to die. So I die, una y otra vez.

The Women Wear Surgical Masks

for three days to mark that they've been
fasting. The fast involves nothing more
than a slice of bread twice a day

& water. They tell each other
this is a luxury because in ten years
the land won't know moisture, even

from the well. On the third day
they rise & husk corn to make
a caldo de res to break the fast later.

This is their monthly mourning.
They march & clouds of dirt rise
from their feet. They carry children

on their shoulders & hang retablos
from their necks. They march
as funeral procession in protest,

all dressed in black. How do you explain
femicide to someone who's never heard
the word? The *New York Times* said the women

look like ghosts, but I've never known
breathing to be so audible. By feeding
the children first, the women break

the fast. No one comes to serve them
& no one cries at this routine. This
is an unbeautiful poem—uncrafted

with sterile diction. I don't want to turn
these women into an aesthetic. I have
failed. That last line break shows I still

want to build tension, but the pain
in my feet from marching with these women,
the sour taste in my mouth from wearing

a surgical mask with these women as a woman,
may never leave me. This poem, my failed
re-creation—their protest a failed resuscitation.

Mi Libro Gore

Inside: missing flyers the size of my palm. Like a clone searching for her original, I paste the negative of each girl's face in a blank book.

You are not your death.

Y ¿How long has she been dead? Y
o ¿Dónde están sus dientes? o
u ¿Do you recognize her shoes? u
   ¿Tienes la misma camisa?
a ¿Missing, for how long? a
r ¿Tiene hijos?
e ¿Was she a prostitute? r
   ¿Vive en Anapra? e
n ¿Why cut under each breast?
o ¿Esta ropa no le vale? n
t ¿Will you get the rape kit? o
   ¿De dónde vienen tantas moscas? t
t ¿Rocks in the vaginal cavity?
h ¿Mordidas por los oídos? h
i ¿More hair 300 ft. away? e
s ¿Una barra en la boca? r
   ¿Puta written in blood?
d ¿Por sus piernas? d
e ¿Whose daughter? e
a ¿De quién es mujer? a
t ¿How should I bag her body? t
h. ¿De dónde son estas esposas? h.

You are not dead.

Macho :: Hembra

Six months later, he was found burnt beyond recognition in the backseat of a car in Ciudad Juárez. He had no teeth. His thumb, index & middle fingers from his right hand, the same hand he used to muffle my screams, were found in the glove compartment. Mutilation turns you into a body unbeckoned. Because his mother refused to give money, they kidnapped him. His father, already missing, imagined dead. Things went wrong in negotiation & they killed him. They left his body in public as lesson: not even dollars can stop hemorrhage.

A Crown of Gold Snakes on My Head

shows I'm dressed for worship. My sins:
so many I lie in losing count. Enter
the cathedral between my thighs
& inside a box & inside the box

red silk. Red silk: my blood. Forgiveness
lets me wear a crown in public.
Forgiveness lets me wear
my blood in pubic. Will you

take my little box of blood? It is blood
I found on a street near the red
looming X of Juárez. Will you take it?
I can't bear it between my thighs

any longer. Please take my blood,
so in silt-stricken water I can die
the way my mother taught me
to dye silk, with the pulped red petals

of a yucca in spring. She taught me
to die, but not to bleed because
a woman's body bleeds without injury.
I lie down in the desert & pull red silk

from the cathedral between my thighs.
I spend all day dying, not from the bite
of a snake on my head, but from the red
silk bridges collapsing between my fingers.

My Brother

climbed a chain-link fence to get to the river. He sat by the river's brush to witness how dry it had become. In the sand he found a tin box & inside he found a knife. He hid the knife in his pocket & when he went to climb the chain-link fence to go home, he cut himself in the thigh. For years he lived with a trench. I'd clean his trench with alcohol & carefully stuff the trench with gauze each morning. When the trench became unbearable I'd sing & use manzanilla to calm his fevered eyes. My brother still lives & his trench has never healed. The trench never healed because we willed it so. The trench hasn't killed him because we willed it so. *Did this trench really happen to your brother?* The trench has happened to every brother I've ever had. I have had many brothers & I have had many trenches. As long as he screams in pain, I know that through the trench we're still alive.

Notes on My Present: A Contrapuntal

I write my body, as border between

this rock & the absence of water.

I cut myself with a scimitar,

as political documentation.

How do you write about the violence

of every man you've ever loved?

Macho, you

breathe bright in the neocolony,

a problem of Empire pulling

the capitalist threads of my border.

Empire: you were so sterile

& shiny with your dead man's coins

& castration, your white roses

& that trash bag full of a Mexican

woman's dark hair. Empire: you

made us hungry for the glint

of machismo, the dim glare

of marianismo. Tonight on TV,

We have some bad hombres here

& we're going to get them out.

When Mexico sends its people,

they're not sending their best.

They're not sending you.

They're sending people

that have lots of problems

& they're bringing those problems to us.

They're bringing drugs. They're bringing

crime. They're rapists.

Mexico's court system [is] corrupt.

I want nothing to do with Mexico

other than to build an impenetrable

WALL & stop them from ripping

off U.S. I love the Mexican people,

but Mexico is not our friend.

They're killing us at the border

45

muted montages of the largest

& they're killing us on jobs & trade.

ICE raid in Texas. I drink

FIGHT! Happy #CincodeMayo!

pink champagne in a hotel bar

The best taco bowls are made

in Trump Tower Grill. I love Hispanics!

& correct the pronunciation of my name.

Macho :: Hembra

This is how macho :: hembra play house. This is how macho :: hembra play love. This is how macho :: hembra crave violence. This is how macho :: hembra purge themselves. These events are related. A man whispers in my ear: I want to break you & I think I am in love. I accept machismo. Hembra is to let men bite your mouth until it bleeds. Hembra is to witness your thighs cut to stars by the thrusts of men. Hembra is to know sex is a blind flicked shut. Machismo is not about the father. Machismo is not about walnuts waiting to be peeled, chiles turned soft, pomegranate thrown on a plate to be served to your macho. Machismo is men as animals hunting: kiss her neck, crack it, still her under your chin.

One Body

Id

Two ids walk into one body & fight over whether to break melon on the kitchen counter & eat it by the fistful, or to throw the melon out a shut window & watch it break on the pavement, stabbed by shards of glass.

Ego

Sorry, for yelling through the speaker at the McDonald's drive-thru. Sorry, for not letting you through the door first. Sorry, I ate the dozen doughnuts in fifteen minutes over the sink. Sorry I sound shrill, sound dumb, sound spacey. Sorry, Mom. I mean, Mamá. I mean, Miss. I mean, never mind.

Superego

Dear body: Cut the melon into slices with the sharpest knife you can find & enjoy the pain you are causing this melon. Stop saying you're sorry, instead feel guilty for being shrill, being dumb, being ditzy, being spacey. Feel guilty because your mom is your mamá is your miss is the one who is guilty for giving you this body with two ids & one ego & one superego who hush-hushes you whole.

There Is No Such Thing as Confession in Latinx Poetry

1. During the Mexican Revolution I set up a lawn chair at the bank of the Río Bravo & watched men kill other men. Near me a woman passed around a bottle of champagne, so I had a glass.

2. He told me to make only rice because the medication made everything taste of chalk, so why make anything more complicated than the food our mothers used to stop our stomachs from speaking to God?

3. His stretch marks are train tracks down his back. In Utah a stranger told him his skin was ugly. When you know hunger, the body can't understand being full & leaves scars to deal with gluttony.

4. In a glass box with a little metal latch I collect my tears. For a place to sleep I will give my tears to you. With just one drop, I promise, they will revive your dying plants.

5. I am a woman who knows how to turn her beauty on & off, how to change its bulb, how to wash her face with white vinegar until it shines like glass.

6. There are days when I feel small & paint miniature rocking chairs as offering to those who have died.

7. I am not I. He is not he. They are not they. We have crossed this bridge that is no one's back, but concrete & metal & wire that will gash us to enjoying the blood in our gums.

Macho :: Hembra

My abuelita sat Chaíto down. Both Chaíto's eyes were black & her handkerchief covered in blood. Chaíto talked of recipes & telenovelas. Chaíto laughed as if her eyes were not red with blood, her face ripe with swelling. When Chaíto left, my abuelita said: *Chaíto's husband shows her love in strange ways, don't let men show you love like that.* My abuelita said: *Climb two hundred stairs to a chapel on our knees to help Chaíto.* My abuelita did this until her knees grew their own shadows. Chaíto came to visit my abuelita again & again, all summer, her eyes two candles melting in the sun. The shadows on my abuelita's knees grew their own bodies. The bruises on Chaíto's face dark as burnt wick.

My intelligent mammal, male
of my species, twin sun to a world
not of my making, you reduce me
to the syrup of the moon, you boil
my bones in the absence of your hands.

::

Mi mamífero inteligente, macho
de mi especie, sol mellizo de un mundo
no de mi creación, me reduces
al jarabe de la luna, hierves
mis huesos en la ausencia de tus manos.

Lorna Dee Cervantes, "A un Desconocido"

You Are a Dark Body

of water with a bed of rock barely visible
from your surface. You are the only dark body

of water in a desert littered with bleeding cactus.
At your collarbones you carry a gulch, held up by a thread

of hair. You travel days drinking only from yourself,
because you are this land's only dark body

of water. At the crease of horizon you find a woman
in bed, her chest wet with saliva, you kick her

off the bed & take her place among its sheets. A man
lies down in bed next to you. He swallows your dark body

of water & gives you a woman's body, a body you've
never known. As a woman, you receive sores from him & through

the sores you breathe & despite the sores you give birth
to a child stillborn for lack of water. You kick the child off

the bed, but it returns in the arms of the woman whose bed
you stole. You cry to be made again into a dark body

of water. The man kicks you off the bed, covers you
with dirt & turns you desert. You cry for a bed he will never

let you sleep in again. You cry for your body's bed
of rock turned desert for lack of water.

I Wait for a Bus

A sign asks: Are you hiding
your pregnancy? I am pregnant

with so many things: black streaks
in the bathtub of a newly rented

apartment, a nose replicated 3×
in bulletproof glass, a book

threaded shut on the mantel.
My womb is full of everything

but a child. My womb the box
to bury their little heads in.

My whole body barren, except
for this lungful of snow. Can you hear

tiny red cans of Coca-Cola grafted
to the branches of my uterus sway

in the wind? Aren't they pretty? Call me,
pretty. I strike each streetlamp

with a match until ribbons
bleed out. On the bus my body

lost another body. What will I do
for all these passengers

with cracked lips? How can I
help them? I'll stare at them—

my eyes hanging
from (con)genital places.

Bad Mother :: Bad Father

You come home with a bottle
of sotol, an apple floating
in its pit. You say the apple grew
inside this bottle & you snapped

it off a branch to bring home
to me. I pour each of us a glass
& smash the bottle to rescue
its tiny fruit. You drink liquor

from the ground until flakes
of glass cut your tongue. In my jaw
I carry the apple—little fruit,
little child—to the yard to hush

its sticky crying. The apple stains
my hands yellow as I slide
its soft flesh down my throat.
When I return to the house

you sniff the corners of my mouth
hungry for any evidence of what
I have done. You say: *You are*
the bad mother. I say: *You are*

the bad father to have brought
this fruit home at all. I drink
& drink, until I root into a tree.
You sell the fruit I bear in bottles.

Receta en El Cajón

INGREDIENTS

Mezcal	Stars	Tripe	Copal	Hen
Dogs	Cow's Feet	Narrow Bones	Oregano	Garlic
Bay Leaves	Onion	Chiles Guajillos	Limes	Salt
Coffee	Mesh Sieve	Tinita	Tortillas	Ladle

DIRECTIONS

1. When your macho comes home gurgling a bottle of mezcal, begin the menudo.

2. He'll whisper: *Te amo chiquitita,* then palm your face to the window. You'll scan for stars made invisible by streetlamps. When he lets you go, laugh: *I've never liked Estrellita.*

3. When he falls asleep at your feet, remember how you disobeyed the song: *Marry an old man, young men like rumba too much.*

4. Cut tripe into ribbons in the sink. Finger curved ridges clean. Tripe, though combed, is a bowel.

5. Light copal in a warm clay bowl until it melts to sap. Make the sign of the cross on your lips, grit its ash against your teeth.

6. In a large pot: tripe, cow's feet, narrow bones, onion, oregano, garlic & salt. Add cold water & simmer all night.

7. Go to bed. Ignore the smell of shit; it will linger in the house for days.

8. Rise with the rooster & wring a hen's neck. Drain the hen of its blood. Hold its clucking still so it doesn't wake your macho. Hang on a hook.

9. Drain the broth of boiled blood w/ a funnel & a tight mesh sieve. Pull any meat from its bones & throw cartilage to the dogs hungry on the patio.

10. Clean chiles of membranes, roast on the comal. Turn each chile soft in a pot of hot water, then grind. Wash your hands with oil made from the rind of a lime.

11. Combine & let simmer: broth, chiles, tripe, bay leaves. Metate y petate.

12. In a bowl: limes. In a shaker: oregano. Both: on the table. The table: floats. Hold it down with a ladle.

13. Wake your macho: provide coffee, provide a tinita.

14. Watch him eat. Your kitchen will grow a film of fat you must clean, the tortillas hard in their wait.

15. *You look tired,* he'll say. *You look worse,* you'll say. Nod & know he'll be home from the orchard late. Pluck feathers from your hanged hen in the yard.

There Is a Bird in My Mouth

I found it on your belly & caught it
with two fingers. I kept the bird
on a little perch behind my ear.

I plucked its feathers, stuffed them
against my jaw like chewing tobacco
& spit the black threads

into a Styrofoam cup. One night
the bird died. Crushed beak, split
bone—we did it. Your heart

jealous, my body disgusted
by the taste of seed & bark—
we didn't want the bird.

We did it over dinner,
you reached into my memory
by placing a finger

in my ear. I placed a hand
in your mouth to catch the bird
& we smashed it

together. This is simple, we did it
& spoke of it with ease. Through
the memory, we killed

the bird that was never ours.
*Now we've become
bird butchers,* you say

& throw the bird's limp body
in the trash. I reach to clasp
your face, but have lost

both my hands. Each finger
disappeared into your pupils,
our little black cruxes.

For My Son Born in La Mariscal

Ciudad Juárez

You bob & spit & bite

at my breast. You are my private

colony of sharp stones. I burn

your umbilical cord to cinders.

Come, meet the spirits. Before

your birth I thought you an eyeball

bruised purple. I have no crib

to leave you in but a box of Maizena

& a blanket of my thick dark hair.

I have done many things to feed your body—

open-legged, dark-thumbed

things. Things for the price of what

I can endure in thirty minutes before

breaking. I know I can't keep you,

but my stillborn, I used the blood

I gave you to wash my legs clean.

Last Night I Was Killed by Man

I woke—& red butterflies spotted
our sheets. With his bare fists man knocked
a seizure into me & then I died. I am back

from that death & watch man tell women
he loves them hour-long in the park. When I died
dead june bugs veiled my face because I let

man put his fingers dark with earth on me.
When I died I hoped they'd call me reina
of something, anything at all. Instead,

man tells bartenders how he licked
my gray cheek like a dog. Death isn't so bad
except being tied to a person. A dust storm

is coming & man doesn't jam the gap under
the door with a towel. There's no one here
to sweep the floors & he doesn't

mind. Late at night he turns animal & hunts
for women to rock him gently:
his mother, his whore, his child.

Criada

Black leather shoes, the only thing
you own that isn't borrowed.
¡Ay thank you, for the gift
of brown welts, black leather shoes!

Miss says: *Five dollars*
to clean the piss off the toilet.
Miss watches as you hold
your breath & scrub.

More bleach, keep cleaning, behind
the seat, get the tiles, says Miss.
Miss keeps her word & gives you
five whole dollars to buy

a pair of earrings on a velour pillow.
You buy gold hoops because
Miss says: *Your head is so little,*
it might float off your shoulders

& fly away. You loop each one
through skin & they're yours.
All you own bruises & cuts your body,
each gold hoop stains your ears green.

¿What can I clean next? you ask.
Miss says: *You see, it's all she wants*
to do, all her little hands are good for.
Miss covers your eyes & spins you:

¿Aren't you happy?
Very jappy, you say wiping pus
from each ear. Miss opens her wallet,
& says: *You mean, very HA-ppy.*

I Am with Child

who eats thin steak still
bleeding. Child sits on my chest,

says, *Cut off my head, please.*
I look for a plastic knife & saw

at child's cheeks. Child screams,
Saw! Saw! Saw! I saw, until

child says, *I want to burst
into a thousand video game pixels.*

I saw until child's blood falls
on my shirt. I carry child

in my rotating arms & call thief
to take child away. Thief comes

& fills child's cuts with gold leaf
he stole from the Catedral

Metropolitana. Thief says child
is holy & child can give

forgiveness. Child looks deep
into the stripes of my pupils

& says, *I do not forgive the bug
on your immigrant tongue.*

I open my mouth, find
my immigrant bug—

a black sore. I clean the knife
of child's blood on my sleeve,

cut the sore free & ask
child what I must do.

Child says, *That sore*
was a gift from your immigrant

mother—welcome, you are
immigrant no more.

Argyria

You swallow silver bullets with a glass of milk until gray
appears on your earlobes & a faint blue moon drapes

itself across your cuticles. A gray that makes you think
of dying as an alien. Not the alien they called you

as a child because you had no papers, but the alien
they called you because your ears are removed

from your head. To eat silver is to get closer
to wealth. To eat silver is to get closer to buying

your mother a new kitchen stove, a car, a sofa
just for napping. Argyria is a skin condition

that has made your blood thicker & darker.
Will argyria turn you toxic? Slide yourself

across the grayscale, let argyria hold you
gainsboro, drip dimgray & sputter

slate. Say: *hold me, argyria, until I become the silver
men mine my #CØCØCØ body for, until I am the silver*

*chain they pull across the necks of their hungry
daughters & feed to their teething sons.*

Marianismo

For Julio Cortázar, Ana Castillo & those who know

+

A shell of teeth,
mother-of-pearl brilliant.
I wash each tooth by hand.
They are the bones
of my daughter still
to fall. A foam collects
in the vitals of the earth
full of teeth. Bones,
from my womb
washed clean with hot
water in a brass tub
& poured beneath
the ocotillo to be burned.

++

Dios te salve, María,
llena eres de gracia,
el Señor es contigo.
Bendita tu eres
entre todas las mujeres
y bendito es el fruto
de tu vientre, Jesús.
Santa María,
Madre de Dios,
ruega por nosotros
pecadores ahora
y en la hora
de nuestra muerte.

+++

No llores, María,
tell no one
of the child. Tell
no one, María,
even when machos
laugh as you hum
to yourself over
the pot of laundry.
Beat each sheet
against stone.
The washing
machine, gone
to rust in the yard.

++++

Que te salves,
María, llena eres
de rajas, estás
sola en este mundo.
Bendito es El entre
todas las mujeres
y bendito es el trabajo
de tu vientre, Jesús.
María, ama de casas,
ruega por nosotros
pecadores ahora y
en la hora de
nuestro nacimiento.

+++++

María, when your macho
comes knocking at the back
gate, turn each light
off. Pretend no one
is home, María. Pretend
you are not home, in your
body. Pretend your body
did not lose pressed
skin & blood. Pretend
you did not rid yourself
of your child, of your
baby, by your body,
your cuerpo. Your body?

++++++

The desert is always
hungry. I break
rock to dirt
with a pick. Sky
breaks in shards.
I wash the child, hope
to hear a scream.
She is dead, but I
carry her, eyes closed,
through the yard &
breathe into her
mouth, which looks
like my mouth.

+++++++
Who is the father,
María? Does it matter
who it was if he
isn't here now?
Does it matter who
it was if he wasn't
here when from
between your legs
you bled into bedding
onto the floor. You made
this baby, it was your
baby. You made it,
it was yours.

++++++++
There is no damp earth
here, only powder
I grind from teeth
to use as dye for thread.
This is my solitary
burial. No macho cares
for the child born but not
breathing. My baby, I tried
to roll myself into a ball
as he kicked to break
teeth, but you would not
stop bleeding, you kept
flooding between my knees.

+++++++++
Dios te dejo,
María, llena eres de
llantos, el Señor
te dejo en el desierto.
Bendita es tu hija,
muerta debajo del
ocotillo, y bendita
es su flor, roja como
la sangre que florece.
Santa María, madre
de la hija muerta
antes de vivir,
ruega, ruega, ruega.

Buen Esqueleto

Life is short & I tell this to mis hijas.
Life is short & I show them how to talk
to police without opening the door, how
to leave the social security number blank
on the exam, I tell this to mis hijas.
This world tells them I hate you every day
& I don't keep this from mis hijas
because of the bus driver who kicks them out
onto the street for fare evasion. Because I love
mis hijas, I keep them from men who'd knock
their heads together just to hear the chime.
Life is short & the world is terrible. I know
no kind strangers in this country who aren't
sisters a desert away & I don't keep this
from mis hijas. It's not my job to sell
them the world, but to keep them safe
in case I get deported. Our first
landlord said with a bucket of bleach
the mold would come right off. He shook
mis hijas, said they had good bones
for hard work. *Mi'jas, could we make this place
beautiful?* I tried to make this place beautiful.

The Hunt

For Lydia Mendoza, La Alondra de la Frontera

A macho told me to close my legs
or he'd take me to a dark room
& make me cry. I closed
my legs. He asked me
to give him a kiss. I gave him
a kiss. I was a child. I could not stop
crying & he could not understand why.

::

My father was a ghost
in our house. He would not speak
for days, then drop a glass of water
on the kitchen floor. My mother swept up
his shatters & buried them in the yard.

::

A macho put his hands on my knees,
then became tarantula, traveled
up my skirt. I didn't scream.
I felt chosen. I was thirteen. I felt lucky
he had chosen me to be hunted.

::

Machos hunt to watch women
in orgasm. Not because they like
to see women in pleasure,
but because they like to watch
women close to death.

::

Machos don't know what it is
to give birth
to the dead. Machos know

pleasure through release. Machos
hunt to give pain & to witness
pleasure. To testify:
the resurrection of the body.

::

I will not apologize
for my desire to love a macho
who could crush my skull
with his bare fists.

::

I apologize to a daughter
for telling her to close her legs.
Machos are hunting, always hunting
to see women close to death.

::

I work two jobs & still come home
to an empty pantry. I am a bad woman
when I can't feed hunger. My labor:
the taste of bleach after an alacrán stings my feet.

::

I write to machos & never
send my letters. In the age
of Los Zetas, I am a lucky
hembra: I have a language
to write of the violence of machos.

::

I watch the azahars grow into lemons
machos pull too early from their branches.
I slice each lemon's rind into translucent
sheets & place each little sun under
the tongue of my macho who eats & eats.

NOTES

"I Am à la Mode" & "She Is à la Mode" were published as part of the PINTURA: PALABRA portfolio in the *Western Humanities Review.* Though I was not a part of the larger workshops that took place in Salt Lake City, I was invited to contribute through the generosity of Francisco Aragón, Carolina Ebeid, Michael Mejia & Fred Arroyo. "I Am à la Mode" and "She Is à la Mode" are both after Asco's No Movie *À la Mode* (photographer Harry Gamboa Jr.), 1976, printed 2010, chromogenic print.

"Aesthetic Translation" includes text in italics from "Drug War on Doorsteps All Over Ciudad Juárez" by Stephen Holden & "Ciudad Juárez, a Border City Known for Killing, Gets Back to Living" by Damien Cave, both published in the *New York Times.*

"Ixmiquilpan, Hidalgo, México" was written in response to a research trip I made with my partner, José Ángel Maldonado, in which we participated in a border crossing simulation called La Caminata Nocturna. Maldonado's article on this trip, titled "Thanatourism, Caminata Nocturna & the Complex Geopolitics of Mexico's Parque EcoAlberto," was published in *Southern Communication Journal* 80, no. 4.

"In the Culture of Now" has lines from the song "Luna Lunera," based on a Spanish children's rhyme, though I grew up most familiar with the version sung by Eydie Gormé y Los Panchos.

"The Women Wear Surgical Masks" is based on a series of protests that took place in El Paso–Juárez, approximately 2008–2012, in which women wore surgical masks to mark that they were part of a hunger strike against femicide.

"Mi Libro Gore" takes its title from the film *Voy a Explotar,* in which protagonist Román Hernández keeps a book of newspaper clippings that document acts of violence by his father, a corrupt PRI party politician, against his local community.

"Notes on My Present: A Contrapuntal" contains statements by President Donald Trump.

"Receta en El Cajón" references advice given to young women in the song "La Cortina."

"Marianismo" contains the prayer Hail Mary in Spanish.

"Buen Esqueleto" was written as an alternative undocumented Latinx perspective to Maggie Smith's viral poem "Good Bones."

ACKNOWLEDGMENTS

I want to thank the editors of the following journals who first published poems that appear in this book, many in earlier forms:

The Academy of American Poets' Poem-a-Day, *The Awl, Bennington Review, Boston Review, Boulevard, BuzzFeed, Gulf Coast, HEArt, Indiana Review, Kenyon Review, Los Angeles Review of Books, NACLA, The Nation, Pleiades, Poetry, Tinderbox, Tin House, The Volta, Waxwing, West Branch, Western Humanities Review,* and *Zócalo Public Square.* The poem "One Body" was republished by *Poetry Daily.* The poem "Receta en El Cajón" (under the title "Menudo") was anthologized in *Vinegar & Char: Verse from the Southern Foodways Alliance.*

Thank you to the women of my family who have had to negotiate around the egos of men their entire lives. Te quiero en esta vida y en la muerte: Dolores, Felicidad, Marxina, Pilar, Clara, Betty & Elaine.

José Ángel Maldonado, mi amorsito corazón, we fell in love knowing our connection was deeper than this life, thank you for helping me explore my piquetitos.

Dana Levin, my forever mentor, you answered obscure e-mails about the difficulties of writing a second book at all hours with a kind word & endless resources. Dana, I bow to you in gratitude.

Javier Zamora, thank you for being the first person to look at this book & for believing in it when I was afraid of what I had created. Thank you, Marcelo Hernández Castillo, for being a true friend. Chelo y Javi, I'm proud to be living, learning & writing alongside you at this crucial time. Thank you for never turning me away.

Thank you for your friendship: Jimena Lucero, Trevor Dane Ketner, Katie Pryor, Benjamin Garcia, Carolina Ebeid, Casandra López, Tanaya Winder, Mario Alejandro Ariza, Ada Limón, Natalie Diaz, Eloisa Amezcua, Rosa Alcalá, Pablo Peschiera, Willy Palomo & Phillip B. Williams.

Thank you, my CantoMundo familia: Deborah Paredez, Celeste Guzmán Mendoza, Carmen Giménez Smith, Amy Sayre Baptista, Urayoán Noel,

Anthony Cody, David Campos, Ángel García, Lauren Espinoza, Beca Alderete Baca & everyone who has ever held me at LlantoMundo.

Eduardo Corral & Rigoberto González, you two are magic makers. Thank you for reaching out to me when I was alone writing in my kitchen. Francisco Aragón, thank you for seeing potential in me and my work.

Lannan Foundation, I was unconvinced anyone read my little poems until I got a phone call from Martha Jessup that forever changed my world. Thank you for giving me the gift of time. This project & the next would never have been possible without you.

Thank you, Westminster College & Natasha Sajé, for the opportunity to be your Poet-in-Residence while working on early versions of this book. Kevin Martínez, gracias por toda la pachanga, eres familia.

Finally, Michael Wiegers, you are one of the most generous souls I've ever met. I will live forever in gratitude that you not only accepted this collection for Copper Canyon Press, but called me, excited to engage with it. That kind of excitement for a poet's work is why Copper Canyon is more than just a press, it's a home. Emily Grise, Laura Buccieri, Elaina Ellis, Rio Cortez, John Pierce, George Knotek, Joseph Bednarik, Sara Ritter & everyone at Copper Cañón will always have a bed, a meal & poems at my house.

And to all of the women of the world who suffer in silence: Nos Queremos Vivas. Queremos tus historias, tu sabiduría, tu fuerza de género. You are enough.

Natalie Scenters-Zapico is a fronteriza from the sister cities of El Paso, Texas, USA, and Ciudad Juárez, Chihuahua, México. She is the author of *The Verging Cities,* winner of the PEN America/Osterweil Award and Great Lakes Colleges Association New Writers Award. Scenters-Zapico has won fellowships from CantoMundo and Lannan Foundation and was awarded a Ruth Lilly and Dorothy Sargent Rosenberg Poetry Fellowship from the Poetry Foundation. She is a professor of literature at Bennington College.

Lannan Literary Selections

For two decades Lannan Foundation has supported the publication and distribution of exceptional literary works. Copper Canyon Press gratefully acknowledges their support.

LANNAN LITERARY SELECTIONS 2019

Jericho Brown, *The Tradition*

Deborah Landau, *Soft Targets*

Paisly Rekdal, *Nightingale*

Natalie Scenters-Zapico, *Lima :: Limón*

Matthew Zapruder, *Father's Day*

RECENT LANNAN LITERARY SELECTIONS FROM
COPPER CANYON PRESS

Sherwin Bitsui, *Dissolve*

Marianne Boruch, *Cadaver, Speak*

John Freeman, *Maps*

Jenny George, *The Dream of Reason*

Ha Jin, *A Distant Center*

Deborah Landau, *The Uses of the Body*

Maurice Manning, *One Man's Dark*

Rachel McKibbens, *blud*

W. S. Merwin, *The Lice*

Aimee Nezhukumatathil, *Oceanic*

Camille Rankine, *Incorrect Merciful Impulses*

Paisley Rekdal, *Imaginary Vessels*

Brenda Shaughnessy, *So Much Synth*

Frank Stanford, *What About This: Collected Poems of Frank Stanford*

Ocean Vuong, *Night Sky with Exit Wounds*

C.D. Wright, *Casting Deep Shade*

Javier Zamora, *Unaccompanied*

Ghassan Zaqtan (translated by Fady Joudah), *The Silence That Remains*

Poetry is vital to language and living. Since 1972, Copper Canyon Press has published extraordinary poetry from around the world to engage the imaginations and intellects of readers, writers, booksellers, librarians, teachers, students, and donors.

WE ARE GRATEFUL FOR THE MAJOR SUPPORT PROVIDED BY:

THE PAUL G. ALLEN
FAMILY FOUNDATION

CULTURE

Anonymous (3)

Jill Baker and Jeffrey Bishop

Anne and Geoffrey Barker

Donna and Matt Bellew

John Branch

Diana Broze

The Beatrice R. and Joseph A. Coleman Foundation, Inc.

Laurie and Oskar Eustis

Mimi Gardner Gates

Nancy Gifford

Gull Industries, Inc. on behalf of William True

The Trust of Warren A. Gummow

Petunia Charitable Fund and advisor Elizabeth Hebert

Bruce Kahn

Phil Kovacevich and Eric Wechsler

Lakeside Industries, Inc.
on behalf of Jeanne Marie Lee

Maureen Lee and Mark Busto

TO LEARN MORE ABOUT UNDERWRITING
COPPER CANYON PRESS TITLES,
PLEASE CALL 360-385-4925 EXT. 103

WE ARE GRATEFUL FOR THE MAJOR SUPPORT PROVIDED BY:

Rhoady Lee and Alan Gartenhaus

Peter Lewis

Ellie Mathews and Carl Youngmann as The North Press

Hank Meijer

Gregg Orr

Gay Phinny

Suzie Rapp and Mark Hamilton

Emily and Dan Raymond

Jill and Bill Ruckelshaus

Kim and Jeff Seely

Richard Swank

Dan Waggoner

Barbara and Charles Wright

Caleb Young as C. Young Creative

The dedicated interns and faithful volunteers
of Copper Canyon Press

The Chinese character for poetry is made up of two parts: "word" and "temple." It also serves as pressmark for Copper Canyon Press.

This book is set in Farnham, designed by Christian Schwartz. The book title is set in Tiffany, designed by Ed Benguiat. Book design by VJB/Scribe. Printed on archival-quality paper.